Everyday Heroes
Wilma Rudolph,
George Washington Carver,
& Jane Addams

Cathy Cotton

Series Editor • Mark Pearcy

Contents

Three American Heroes

Wilma Rudolph, George Washington Carver, and Jane Addams are all **heroes.**

Wilma Rudolph

George Washington Carver

Jane Addams

Wilma Rudolph

Wilma Rudolph was born in 1940. She got sick when she was four years old. She could not move one leg.

> "My doctors told me I would never walk again. My mother told me I would. I believed my mother."
> — Wilma Rudolph

Rudolph wanted to walk. Her family helped her. Rudolph could walk with a brace when she was 8. Rudolph could run without a brace when she was 12.

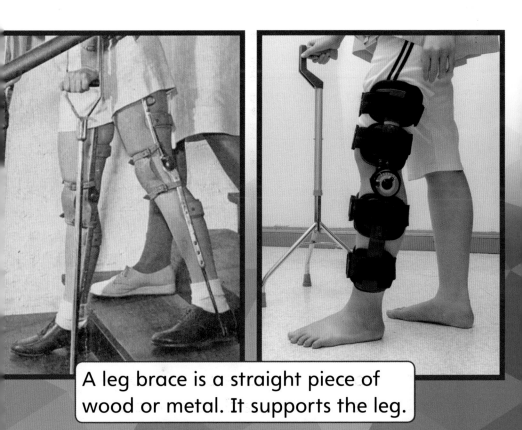

A leg brace is a straight piece of wood or metal. It supports the leg.

The Olympics

Rudolph worked with a running **coach.** She won a bronze medal in the 1956 Olympics.

She won three gold medals in the 1960 Olympics.

Wilma Rudolph won the 1960 Olympic 100-meter race. It took her 11 seconds.

Wilma Rudolph **inspired** people all over the world.

Wilma Rudolph became a teacher and a coach. She helped other athletes.

George Washington Carver

George Washington Carver was born in the 1860s. He and his parents were **enslaved** persons. His owners were Moses and Susan Carver.

Slavery ended in 1865. But George stayed with the Carvers.

Carver was African American. He was not allowed to go to school. Susan Carver taught him to read and write.

Carver at work in his lab

From Farmer to Teacher

Carver became a farmer. He wanted to help plants grow well.

Later, Carver was allowed into a college. He studied farming. He helped other farmers.

Carver used a wagon like this. He put plants in it and taught other farmers about them.

Some farmers only planted cotton. After many years, the soil was not good. Carver told the farmers to plant different things. This would help the soil.

Many farmers started to grow peanuts. Carver invented lots of ways to use peanuts. He was called the Peanut Man.

Jane Addams

Jane Addams was born in 1860. She had a back problem. She was in the hospital a lot. But she was one of the first women to go to university.

Addams went to England with Ellen Gates Starr. They went to a settlement house. It was a place that helped people.

Addams and Starr opened a settlement house in Chicago. It was called Hull House. Thousands of people went there for help.

Hull House closed in 2012.

Addams wanted a peaceful world. She wrote books. She spoke to world leaders. She won the Nobel Peace Prize.

Heroes Never Give Up

Rudolph, Carver, and Addams had problems. But they became heroes. They helped others.

How can you be a hero?

Glossary

coach: a person who teaches others how to be good at a sport

enslaved: forced to give up one's freedom and work for others with no pay

hero: a person who is brave and does good things for others

inspire: to help someone want to do something special

Index